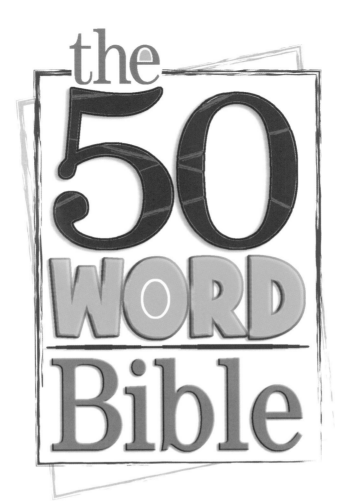

# Dan Miley

**Legacy Press**®
LegacyPressKids.com

Presented to:

_____

By:

_____

Date:

_____

# THE 50 WORD BIBLE

© 2013 by Daniel Miley, first printing
ISBN 10:  1-58411-144-5
ISBN 13:  978-1-58411-144-3
Legacy reorder # LP48751
JUVENILE NONFICTION / Religion / Christian / General


Legacy Press
P.O. Box 261129
San Diego, CA 92196
www.LegacyPressKids.com

Illustrator:  Andy Catling

*Printed in the United States of America*

*For Erin and Rachel–*
*No dad could ask for more*

# In the beginning

God's power

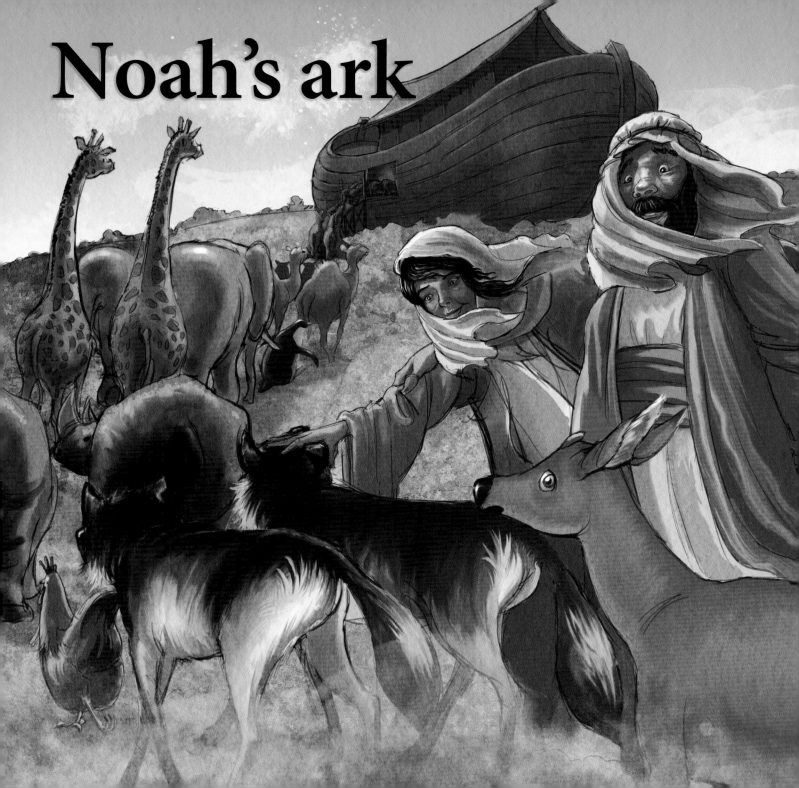

# Noah's ark

# Babel's tower

# Abraham trusts

# Joseph leads

Tablets guide

# Manna feeds

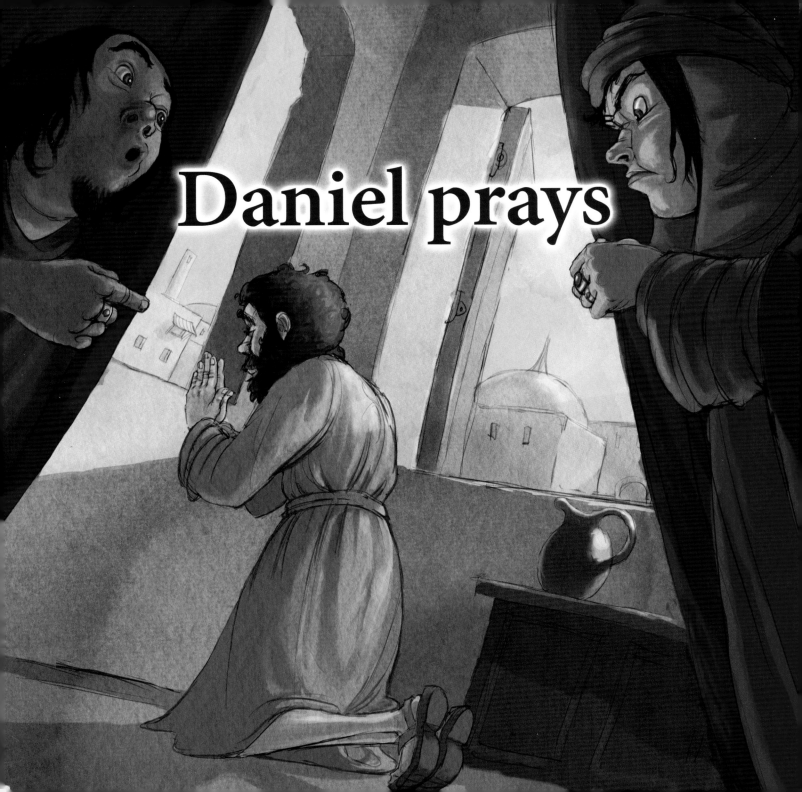

Daniel prays

# Hannah's wish

David's stone

Jonah's fish

# Humble manger

Savior's birth

Peace on Earth

Jesus heals

# Demons flee

Deaf hear

# Blind see

# Burial place

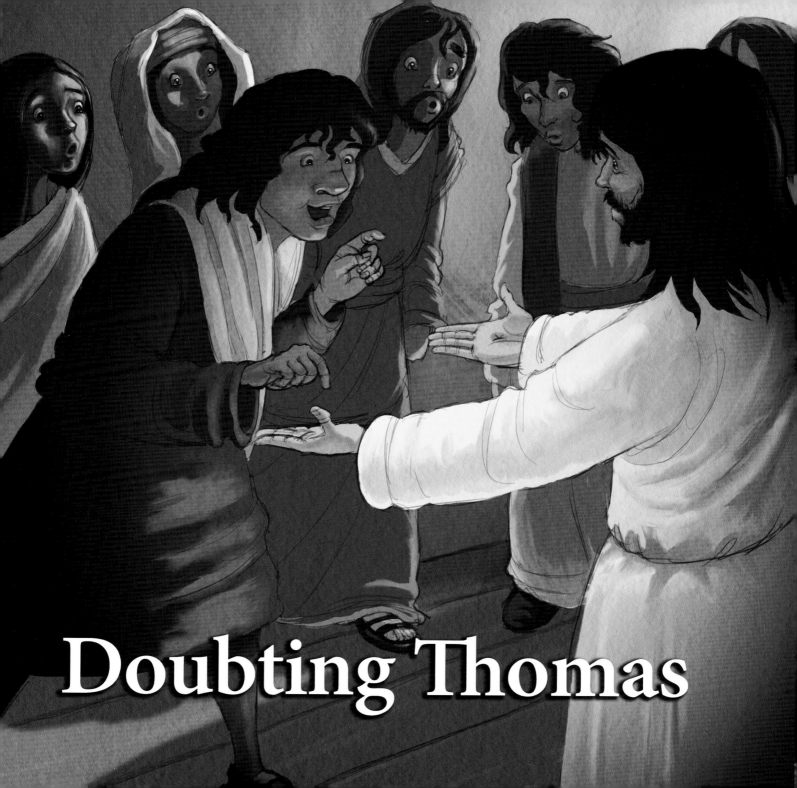

# Doubting Thomas

# Amazing grace!

# Find it in the Bible

## OLD TESTAMENT

# Find it in the Bible
## NEW TESTAMENT

Humble manger.....................................Luke 2:1-5

Savior's birth .......................................Luke 2:6-7

Angels sing .........................................Luke 2:8-14

Peace on Earth .....................................Matthew 2:1-2, 7-11

Jesus heals ..........................................John 11:38-44

Demons flee .........................................Mark 5:1-13

Deaf hear ............................................Mark 7:31-37

Blind see .............................................Mark 10:46-52

Rugged cross ........................................Luke 23:32-43

Burial place .........................................John 20:11-18

Doubting Thomas ..................................John 20:24-29

Amazing grace! .....................................John 3:16

The Bible is filled with **exciting stories** and **brave heroes.** Learn more by visiting 50WordBible.com for fun activities and adventures created just for **YOU!**